100 BEST SONGS OF THE 20'S AND 30'S

100 BEST SONGS
OF THE
20's AND 30's

INTRODUCTION BY

RICHARD RODGERS

Bonanza Books, New York

a division of Crown Publishers
One Park Avenue
New York, N.Y. 10016

Copyright © MCMLXXIII by Warner Bros. Publications Inc.
Library of Congress Catalog Card Number: 73-75348
All rights reserved.
This edition is published by Bonanza Books,
a division of Crown Publishers, Inc.,
by arrangement with Harmony Books.
b c d e f g h
Bonanza Books 1977

ACKNOWLEDGMENTS

The Publishers wish to thank Irving Brown, Bruce Harris and Linda Sunshine for their assistance in the production of this book.

DEDICATION

100 BEST SONGS OF THE 20'S AND 30'S is dedicated to the composers and lyricists in this book who have kept America singing.

PUBLISHER'S NOTE

Because of copyright ownership, it was not possible to include some songs that would otherwise have been chosen. Nevertheless, all the songs represented here are among the best of the 20's and 30's.

TABLE OF CONTENTS

INDEXES

INTRODUCTION

by RICHARD RODGERS

A song is a lot of things. But, first of all, a song is the voice of its times. Setting words to music gives them weight, makes them somehow easier to say. And it helps them to be remembered. It may be that we can sing what we often cannot say, whether it be from shyness, fear, lack of the right words or the passion or dramatic gift to express them. More souls have rallied to more causes by the strains of music than by straining rhetoric. Surely more Frenchmen's hopes of liberation were kept alive by the clandestine playing of the *Marseillaise* than by radioed promises of help during the dark days of Nazi occupation. And *Happy Days Are Here Again* buoyed up the flagging spirits of the Depression years long before it became the "official" 1964 Democratic party campaign song.

Music, too, is the "food of love." We show our love for God by singing hymns to His praise. Love of country is shown in its national anthem; of old school ties in the *alma mater*. And our love for each other is never so eloquently expressed as it is in music . . . in the romantic love song, a genre of popular expression that reached its zenith in the years between 1920 and 1940: the period covered in this songbook.

Music evokes memories of the past, speaks in tones of the present, and inspires the future. The music of the Twenties and Thirties represents, really, the voices of *two* times, separated by a single day late in 1929—the day of the Great Wall Street Crash. In the Twenties people hummed happily while clipping coupons on a collision course with the Thirties. High living, the Bees' Knees and speak-easies turned overnight into dour soup kitchens, plummeting hemlines and the escapism of Shirley Temple movies. But the music of these two decades represented two sides of the same coin. The millionaire-on-margin of 1927 was singing *Brother, Can You Spare a Dime?* in 1932 with the same enthusiasm he formerly reserved for the discovery of a new chorine to shower with furs and costly baubles. Even as songs beat out the rhythm of the present they are tempered with the sweet nostalgia of the past. And they drum up visions of things to come. They log the temper of an entire era.

The Twenties sang of carefree nights and the frenetic days that rushed headlong into the nightmare and fantasy of the Thirties. Both had their reality; both voiced it. This was a score of years in which love grew from an idle and pleasant pastime into a vital avocation—romance. Bread lines seemed less burdensome if one could sing. Somehow, political chaos was less unsettling if you hummed through its storms. And Armageddon couldn't threaten us if we kept whistling *Bye Bye Blackbird*.

The history of the world has been written in music. I am proud to have been a part of its most exciting chapters. I am happy that some of my favorite melodies have helped to chronicle one of America's most fascinating generations. And I am delighted that many of them have been set down between the covers of this book.

Music is something else, too: it is the universal language. It will speak for itself on the following pages.

THE TWENTIES

CHARLESTON FOX TROT
DANCE DIRECTIONS
BY
OSCAR DURYEA, "AMERICAN AUTHORITY ON MODERN DANCES"
The Ballroom, Hotel Des Artistes, One West 67th Street, New York.

To learn this dance, first practice the Charleston step—Place the feet as in illustration No. 1, man's left foot behind the right, left toe at the heel of the right, both toes turned out,—his partner's right foot in front of her left, her right heel at the toe of her left foot, both toes turned out.

The man raise the left foot and at the same time rise on the toe of the right, turn both toes in, twisting on the ball of the right foot —his partner raise her right foot, and at the same time rise on her left toe, twisting on the ball of her left foot, turn both toes in, as in illustration No. 2. For 4/4 time music, in counting Fox Trot, count and,

With the feet in this position, twist both toes out, with the man's left heel in front at his right toe—his partner's right heel in front at her left toe. For 4/4 time music, in counting Fox Trot, count 1.

Man raise his left foot at the same time rise on the ball of the right and twist both toes in, then put left foot behind right, and on the balls of both feet twist both toes out—his left toe behind at the right heel—his partner raise her right foot, at the same time rise on the ball of her left foot and twist both toes in, then put her right foot in front and on the balls of both feet turn both toes out —her right toe in front, at her left heel. For Fox Trot, count and 2. This is the SINGLE CHARLESTON and is done on one side with one foot (the same one) moving forward and backward. After practicing with the foot described, then practice with the other foot, moving it forward and backward with the same movements and counts. A toddle movement (a double rise or jiggle of the body up and down) is taken throughout all the "CHARLESTON" steps, on the foot on which the weight is.

For the DOUBLE CHARLESTON start as before, the left foot for the man, the right for his partner, and take the count "and 1" as before, then step back on the left foot for the man and on the right foot forward for his partner, putting the weight on it, but doing the turning in and out and the toddle with the weight on the left behind for the man, his partner with the weight on her right in front. Count and 2. Then the man "CHARLESTON" with the right foot, moving it back behind the left foot and forward again in front, finishing with the weight on the right foot in front of the left—his partner moves the left foot in front of the right and back with the same foot, finishing with her left foot in front of the right with the weight on it, Count and 3, and 4

FOX TROT ROUTINES WITH SINGLE AND DOUBLE CHARLESTON STEPS

ROUTINE I. Directions for the man, his partner does the same but with the opposite foot in the opposite direction. Walk 4 steps forward, commencing with the left foot, count 1, 2, 3, 4. Then SINGLE CHARLESTON STEPS with the left foot moving forward and backward twice, count and 5, and 6, and 7, and 8 — — 4 measures.

ROUTINE II. Walk 4 steps forward, commencing with the left foot, count 1, 2, 3, 4. Then DOUBLE CHARLESTON with the left foot moving forward and backward, then the right foot backward and forward, count and 5, and 6, and 7, and 8 — — 4 measures.

ROUTINE III. Walk 2 steps forward, commencing with the left foot, count 1, 2, then 3 short quick steps to the left side, with the left, right and left foot (step, close step) finishing with a "kick up" with the right foot from the knee (see illus. No. 4) as the third step is taken on the left foot, count 3 and 4, and repeat the 3 quick steps to the right side with the right, left and right foot, finishing with the "kick up" with the left foot, count 5 and 6 and, then a SINGLE CHARLESTON STEP with the left foot moving forward and backward, count 7 and 8 and — — — — 4 measures.

ROUTINE IV. Repeat ROUTINE III — — — — — — — 4 measures.

NOTE: Discretion should be used as to how pronounced the CHARLESTON "kick up," and "toddle" movements are made for ballroom dancing.

HARMS, Inc. - - 62 West 45th Street, N. Y. C.

AVALON
FOX TROT SONG

Lyric and Music by
AL JOLSON
and VINCENT ROSE

Arr. by J. BODEWALT LAMPE

Ev - 'ry morn-ing mem-'ries stray .... A-cross the
Just be - fore I sail'd a - way .... She said the

sea where fly - ing fish - es play _____
word I long'd to hear her say _____

And as the night is fall - ing
I ten - der - ly ca - ress'd her

I find that I'm re - call - ing
Close to my heart I press'd her

That bliss - ful
Up - on that

all en - thrall - ing day _____
gold - en yes - ter - day _____

CHORUS *semplice*

I found my love in A - va - lon ____ Be -

-side ____ the bay ____ I

left my love in A - va - lon ____ and

sail'd ____ a - way ____ I

5

dream of her and A - va - lon _____ From

dusk _____ 'til dawn _____ And

so I think I'll trav- el on _____ To A -

va = lon   I -lon _____

AIN'T WE GOT FUN

SONG

Lyric by
GUS KAHN
& RAYMOND B. EGAN

Music by
RICHARD A. WHITING

CHORUS

BABY FACE

Words and Music by
BENNY DAVIS and
HARRY AKST

CHORUS

BA - BY FACE_ You've got the cut-est lit-tle BA - BY FACE_ There's not an - oth-er one could take your place._ BA - BY FACE_ My poor heart_ is jump-in', You shure have start - ed some-thin' BA - BY FACE;_ I'm up in heav-en when I'm in your fond em - brace,____ I did-n't need a shove_'Cause I just fell in love_ With your pret - ty BA - BY FACE.____ FACE.____

IF I COULD BE WITH YOU

By HENRY CREAMER
& JIMMY JOHNSON

I'm so blue I don't know what to do
All dressed up but still no-where to go

All day through I'm pin-ing just for you I did wrong when I
How I wish that I could see a show Here I wait with no-

CHORUS

14

I'm Just Wild About Harry

Words and Music by
NOBLE SISSLE and
EUBIE BLAKE
A.S.C.A.P.

*Diagrams for Guitar, Symbols for Ukulele and Banjo

must be a girl___   I've found my mate__   By kind-ness of fate.___
girl of all girls,___   I'm his i-deal,__   How hap-py I feel.___

REFRAIN

I'm just wild__ a-bout Har - ry_____   and Har-ry's wild__ a-bout

me._____ The heav'n - ly bliss - es of his kiss - es

fill me with ec - sta - sy _____ He's sweet just like__ choc'-late

Carolina In The Morning

Lyric by
GUS KAHN

Music by
WALTER DONALDSON

May-be there's noth-ing in wish-ing, But, speak-ing of wish-ing I'll say:
What could be sweet-er than dream-ing, Just dream-ing and drift-ing a - way.

Noth - ing could be fin - er than to be in Car - o - lin - a in the

morn - - ing, No - one could be sweet - er than my

sweet - ie when I meet her in the morn - - ing.

But-ter-flies all flut-ter up and kiss each lit-tle but-ter-cup at dawn - -

ing, If I had A-lad-din's lamp for on-ly a day,—

I'd make a wish and here's what I'd say:— Noth-ing could be fin-er than to

be in Car-o-lin-a in the morn - -ing. ing.

My Buddy

Lyric by
GUS KAHN

Music by
WALTER DONALDSON

*Diagrams for Guitar, Symbols for Ukulele and Banjo

REFRAIN

Valse moderato
Rubato

Nights are long since you went a-way, I think a-bout you all thru the day My Bud-dy,_____ my Bud-dy,_____ No Bud-dy quite so true._____

That we must part, you and I._____
Miss-ing your smile and and your song._____

BARNEY GOOGLE

REGISTERED U. S. PATENT OFFICE

Copyright, 1923, by King Features Syndicate, Inc. "Great Britain Rights Reserved"

SONG

By BILLY ROSE
& CON CONRAD

Who's the most im - por - tant man this coun - try ev - er
Who's the great - est lov - er that this coun - try ev - er

knew   Who's the man our Pres - i - dents tell
knew   Who's the man that Val - en - tin - o

28

CHARLESTON

Words and Music by
CECIL MACK
& JIMMY JOHNSON

With a pe-cu-liar snap!_____ You may not be a-ble to buck or wing, Fox-trot, two-step, or e-ven sing, If you ain't got re-li-gion, in your feet, You can do this prance and do it neat.

REFRAIN *con spirito*

Charles-ton! Charles-ton! Made in Car-o-lin-a,—

CALIFORNIA
Here I Come
FOX TROT SONG
Ukulele in G

By AL JOLSON,
BUD DE SYLVA
and JOSEPH MEYER

ff well marked

Vamp

dim.

When the win-try winds are blow-ing, And the snow is start-ing in to
An-y one who likes to wan-der, Ought to keep this say-ing in his

fall,_____ Then my eyes turn west-ward, know-ing That's the
mind,_____ "Ab-sence makes the heart grow fon-der," Of the

place I love the best of all._____ Cal-i-for-nia,
good old place you leave be-hind._____ When you've hit the

I've been blue,___ Since I've been a - way from you,___ I can't
trail a while ___ Seems you rare-ly see a smile;___ That's why

wait 'til I get go-ing; ev-en now I'm start-ing in to call Oh,
I must fly out yonder, Where a frown is might-y hard to find! Oh,

Ukulele
in C
REFRAIN

Cal - i - for - nia, here I come___ Right back where I

p-ff

start-ed from ___ Where bowers of flow-ers bloom in the sun ___

34

Each morn-ing at dawn-ing, Bird-ies sing an' ev-'ry-thing. A sun-kist

miss said, "Don't be late"___ That's why I can hard-ly wait___

___ Op - en up that Gold - en Gate___ Cal - i -

-for - nia, here I come _____ come _____

L.H.   ffz

35

HARD HEARTED HANNAH

(The Vamp Of Savannah)

Words and Music by
JACK YELLEN, MILTON AG[...]
BOB BIGELOW and CHAS. BA[...]

tor - ture and kill 'em,   Is her de-light, they   say,____   I
tor - ture and kill 'em,   Is her de-light, they   say,____   An

saw her   at   the sea-shore with a great big pan;__There was Han-nah pour-ing wa-ter on   a
ev-'ning spent with Han-nah sit-ting on your knees,__ Is   like trav-'ling thru A-las-ka in your

drown-ing man,__She's HARD HEART-ED HAN-NAH, The Vamp of Sa-van-nah G.   A.
B.   V. D's;__She's HARD HEART-ED HAN-NAH, The Vamp of Sa-van-nah G.

They call her

A.____

I Wonder What's Become Of Sally?

Words by
JACK YELLEN
A.S.C.A.P.

Music by
MILTON AGER
A.S.C.A.P.

Diagrams for Guitar, Symbols for Ukulele and Banjo

40

INDIAN LOVE CALL

Words by
OTTO HARBACH and
OSCAR HAMMERSTEIN IInd

Music by
RUDOLF FRIML

THE MAN I LOVE

From "Lady Be Good"

Words by
IRA GERSHWIN

French version by
EMELIA RENAUD

Spanish text by
Johnnie Camacho

Music by
GEORGE GERSHWIN

make him stay.
dre la main,
tre - ga - ré.

He'll look at me and smile,
Ses yeux me sou - ri - ront
Qui - zás en su mi - rar,

I'll un-der-stand;
Je com-pren-drai
a-pren-da yo,

And in a lit-tle while
Et sans hé - si - ta - tion
Por-qué fué quees-pe - ré

He'll take my hand;
Je ré-pon-drai.
por es - tc a-mor;

And though it seems ab-surd,
Bien que ce soit fo - lie,
Vi - vien-do sin a - mor,

I know we both won't say a
En-tre nous pas un mot n'est
So-ñan- do siem-pre por los

word.____
dit____
dos.____

May-be I shall meet him Sun-day, May-be Mon-day may-be
Le ver-rais - je lun - di, mar-di? Ou peut être en - core jeu -
Pue-de ser que lle - gue un lu - nes, Pue-de ser que no se -

47

Oh, Lady Be Good!

Words by
IRA GERSHWIN

Music by
GEORGE GERSHWIN

* Diagrams for Guitar, Symbols for
Ukulele and Banjo

I could blos-som out I know, With some-bod-y just like you, so,
If some-bod-y won't re-spond, I'm go-ing to end it all, so,

REFRAIN

p - mf slow and gracefully

Oh, sweet and love-ly la-dy, be good! — Oh la-dy, be good
Oh, sweet and love-ly la-dy, be good! — Oh la-dy, be good —

— to me! — I am so awf'-ly
— to me! — I am so awf'-ly

mis-un-der-stood, — So la-dy be good — to me.
mis-un-der-stood, — So la-dy be good — to me.

Oh,   please have some pit - y ——
This   is tu - lip weath - er ——

I'm all a - lone in this big cit - y   I tell you I'm just a
So let's put two and two to - geth - er   I tell you I'm just a

lone - some babe in the wood —— So   la - dy, be good ——— to
lone - some babe in the wood —— So   la - dy, be good ——— to

me! ——————————   me! —————
me! ——————————   me! —————

ROSE-MARIE

Words by
OTTO HARBACH and
OSCAR HAMMERSTEIN IInd
Spanish text by
Johnnie Camacho

Music by
RUDOLF FRIML

REFRAIN Moderato (molto amabile)

Rose - Ma - rie. I love you! I'm al - ways
Rose - Ma - rie, te quie - ro, Mi sue - ño es

dream - ing of you. No mat - ter what I
a - do - rar - te. Por más que yo he tra -

do, I can't for - get you; Some - times I wish that
ta - do de ol - vi - dar - te, Com - pren - do que sin

I had nev - er met you! And yet if
ti, de pe - na, mue - ro. Y si, tú

54

TEA FOR TWO

Words by
IRVING CAESAR

Music by
VINCENT YOUMANS

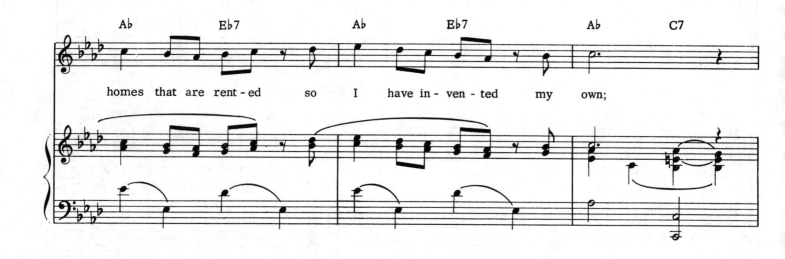

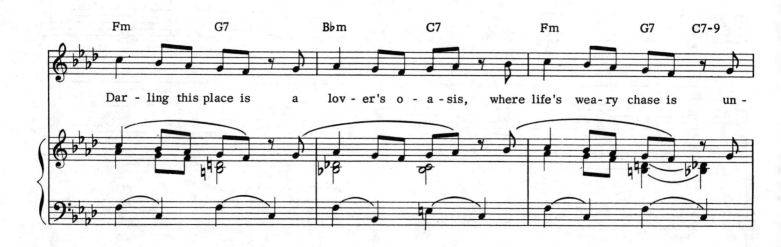

start to bake a sug-ar cake For me to take for all the boys to

see. _____ We will raise a fam - i - ly, A

boy for you, A girl for me, Oh can't you see how hap - py we would

1. be?   **2.** be?

When Day Is Done

Tune Ukulele

B♭ E♭ G C

Words by
B.G. DE SYLVA

Music by
DR. ROBERT KATSCHER

Since you've gone a - way, one thing is clear to me;
Ves - per bells are ring - ing, some where far a - way;

You were dear-er than dear to me,   From the mom-ent you
There's a sil-ver-y star a - way,   At the edge of the

twi - light's dew, My lone - ly heart is sink - ing with the

sun. Al - though I miss your ten - der kiss the

whole day through, I miss you most of all when day is

done! When done!

☆ *Open Strings*

CLAP HANDS!
Here Comes Charley!

Lyric by
BILLY ROSE &
BALLARD MacDONALD

Tune Ukulele

G C E A

Music by
JOSEPH MEYER

Ukulele Arr by MAY SINGHI BREEN

Have you met my good friend
He's the life of ev-'ry

Char-ley? Well you've heard of him no doubt. He's the great big Good Time Char-ley That the
part-y, And he pays and pays and pays; And he cries when they put pad-locks On his

girls all rave a-bout.___ He's as wel-come at a part-y As the flow-ers are in
fav-or-ite ca-fes.___ He's a big man with the la-dies, And a sail-or with his

Spring; An-y-time they see him com-ing, Ev-'ry-one be-gins to sing.
dough. All the cus-tom-ers and wait-ers, When they see him, yell, "Let's Go!"

CHORUS

Clap hands! Here comes Char-ley; Clap hands! Good time Char-ley; Clap hands!
Clap hands! Here comes Char-ley; Clap hands! Good time Char-ley; Clap hands!

Here comes Char-ley now._____ This way – join the part-y;
Here comes Char-ley now._____ This way – meet the dol-lies,

I say – meet Mc-Carth-y; Hey! Hey! Char-ley, take a bow_____
I say – Zieg-field Fol-lies; Hey! Hey! Char-ley, take a bow_____

A

Gin - ger Ale and White Rock for this ta - ble,
See the smile on all those hun-gry fac - - es,

Grab a chair, move o - ver there, And let him sit right next to Ma - ble;
They can tell that he's a buy - er From those wide and o - pen spac - es;

Clap hands! Here comes Char-ley; Clap hands! Good time Char - ley; Clap hands!
Clap hands! Here comes Char-ley; Clap hands! Good time Char - ley; Clap hands!

Here comes Char-ley now._____ now._____
Here comes Char-ley now._____ now._____

A Cup Of Coffee, A Sandwich And You

Words by
BILLY ROSE
and AL DUBIN

Music by
JOSEPH MEYER

love laid in a gar-den 'neath the moon.——

But I don't miss that kind of bliss

What I want is this —————— A cup of

Refrain *(very simply)*
Cof-fee, a sand-wich and you,————— A co-zy

DON'T BRING LULU
SONG

Lyric by
BILLY ROSE
& LEW BROWN

Music by
RAY HENDERSON

SWEET GEORGIA BROWN

By BEN BERNIE,
MACEO PINKARD
& KENNETH CASEY

*Diagrams for Guitar, Symbols for Ukulele and Banjo

CHORUS

No gal made has got a shade On Sweet Geor-gia Brown,

Two left feet but oh so neat has Sweet Geor-gia Brown;

They all sigh and wan-na die For Sweet Geor-gia Brown, I'll tell you just

why, you know I don't lie, Not much!

spoken ad lib.

The Birth Of The Blues

Words by
B. G. DE SYLVA
and LEW BROWN
A.S.C.A.P.

Music by
RAY HENDERSON
A.S.C.A.P.

Diagrams for Guitar, Symbols for Ukulele and Banjo

BYE BYE BLACKBIRD
SONG

Ukulele in D
Tune Uke thus A D F♯ B

when played with Piano. (Tenor Banjo, Mandola,
Guitar etc. play chords marked over diagrams.)

Lyric by
MORT DIXON

Music by
RAY HENDERSON

Do-Do-Do

Words by
IRA GERSHWIN

Music by
GEORGE GERSHWIN

Kay: I re-mem-ber it quite, 'Twas a won-der-ful night!
Jimmy: I can't see that at all True love nev-er should pall.

Jimmy: Oh, how I'd a-dore it, If you would en - core it. Oh,
Kay: I was on-ly teas-ing What you did was pleas-ing. Oh,

Refrain

do, do, do what you've done, done, done be - fore,

ba - by. Do, do, do what I do, do, do a -

don't, don't, don't say it won't, won't, won't come true,
see, see, see lit - tle me, me, me make you

ba - by. My heart be - gins to hum: Dum - de - dum - de -
hap - py. *Kay:* My heart be - gins to sigh Di - de - di - de -

dum - dum - dum, So do, do, do what you've done, done, done be -
di - di - di So do, do, do what you've done, done, done be -

fore.   Oh,
fore.

Mountain Greenery

Words by
LORENZ HART

Music by
RICHARD RODGERS

SOMEONE TO WATCH OVER ME
"QUI ME PROTÉGERA"

Words by
IRA GERSHWIN
French version by
EMELIA RENAUD

Music by
GRORGE GERSHWIN

There's a say-ing old Says that love is blind, Still we're of-ten told "Seek and
Un pro-ver-be dit l'a-mour a-veu-glé, On nous dit aus-si: "Cher-chez

ye shall find". So I'm going to seek A cer-tain lad I've had in mind.
pour trou-ver" Je cher-che ce gail-lard qui m'est res-té dans l'i-dée

Look-ing ev-'ry-where, Have-n't found him yet; He's the big af-fair I can-
Re-gar-dant par-tout sans le ren-con-trer; C'est un gars que je ne puis

not for-get. On-ly man I ev-er Think of with re-gret.
ou-bli-er. Le seul homme à qui je pense a-vec re-gret.

I'd like to add his in-i-tial to my mon-o-gram.
Mon nom pour ses i-ni-tia-les je le chan-ge-rais.

Tell me, where is the shep-herd for this lost lamb.
Pour la bre-bis per-due où est le ber - ger?

AIN'T SHE SWEET

Words by
JACK YELLEN
A.S.C.A.P.

Music by
MILTON AGER
A.S.C.A.P.

HALLELUJAH!

Words by
LEO ROBIN and
CLIFFORD GREY

Music by
VINCENT YOUMANS

107

I'm Looking Over A Four Leaf Clover

Lyric by
MORT DIXON

Music by
HARRY WOODS

CHORUS

I'M LOOK-ING O-VER A FOUR LEAF CLO-VER that I o-ver-looked be-fore;_____ One leaf is sun-shine, the sec-ond is rain,_ Third is the ros-es that grow in the lane,_ No need ex-plain-ing, the one re-main-ing Is some-bo-dy I a-dore._____ I'M LOOK-ING O-VER A FOUR LEAF CLO--VER that I o-ver-looked be-fore._____ -fore._____

My Heart Stood Still
(Martin and Sandy)

Words by
LORENZ HART

Music by
RICHARD RODGERS

Martin: I laughed at sweet - hearts
Sandy: Through all my school - days

I met at schools;
I hat - ed boys;

All in - dis - creet hearts
Those Ap - ril - Fool days

110

And then my heart stood still!

My feet could step and walk, My lips could move and talk,

And yet my heart stood still! Though not a

sin-gle word was spok-en, I could tell you knew,—

Sometimes I'm Happy

Tune Ukulele

G C E A

Words by
IRVING CAESAR

Music by
VINCENT YOUMANS

He: Ev - 'ry day seems
He: Stars are smil - ing at me

like a year,
from your eyes

Sweet - heart, when you
She: Sun - beams now there will be

are not near.

in the skies.

She: All that you claim must be true For I'm

He: Tell me that you will be true! *She:* That will

mf *espressivo molto*

just the same as you:

all de-pend on you dear!

rall.

rall.

Refrain (*slowly*)

p-mf

p-mf

Some-times I'm hap-py, Some-times I'm blue,—

My dis - po - si - tion de - pends on you,—

I nev - er mind the rain from the skies,—

If I can find the sun in your eyes.—

Some - times I love you, Some - times I

STOUTHEARTED MEN

(Including U.S. Navy version)

Words by
OSCAR HAMMERSTEIN IInd

SIGMUND ROMBERG

Give me some men who are stout-heart-ed men who will fight for the right they a-
Give me some men who are stout-heart-ed men who will fight for the right they a-

dore. Start me with ten, who are stout-heart-ed men and I'll
dore. Give me some men who will fight like the men who have

soon give you ten thou-sand more, Oh! Shoul-der to shoul-der and
fought in the na-vy be-fore! Oh! Give me some guns for the

bold-er and bold-er they grow as they go to the fore!
stout-heart-ed sons of the ones who have won ev-'ry war!

STRIKE UP THE BAND!

Words by
IRA GERSHWIN

Music by
GEORGE GERSHWIN

'S WONDERFUL

Words by
IRA GERSHWIN

Music by
GEORGE GERSHWIN

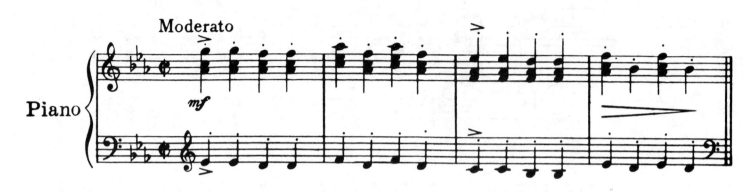

Life has just be - gun. Jack has found his Jill,
Don't mind tell - ing you, In my hum - ble fash,

Don't know what you've done, But I'm all a - thrill.
That you thrill me through With a ten - der pash.

THOU SWELL

Duet
(Sandy and Martin)

Words by
LORENZ HART

Music by
RICHARD RODGERS

Diagrams for Guitar, Symbols for Ukalele and Banjo

130

Are you too wist-full to care,— Do — say you — care to
More thou wilt tell to San - dy.— Thou — art dan-dy; Now —

— say; "Come near lad." You are so grace - ful,
— art thou my knight. Thine arms are mar - tial;

have you. wings? You have a face full of nice things;
Thou hast grace; My cheek is part - ial to thy face;

You have no speak - ing voice, dear, With ev-'ry word it sings.—
And if thy lips grow wea - ry, Mine are their rest - ing place.—

I WANNA BE LOVED BY YOU

Words by
BERT KALMAR

Music by
HERBERT STOTHART
and HARRY RUBY

Let's Do It
(Let's Fall In Love)

Words and Music by
COLE PORTER

Symbols for Ukulele, Guitar and Banjo.

138

Lith - u - an - i - ans and Letts do it,— Let's do it,—
Ev - en laz - y Jel - ly - fish do it,— Let's do it,—

Let's fall in— love.——————— The Dutch in old Am - ster -
Let's fall in— love.——————— E - lect - ric eels, I might—

dam do it,— Not to men - tion the Finns Folks in Si -
add, do it,— Though it shocks 'em I know. Why ask if—

- am do it,— Think of Si-am-ese twins. Some Ar-gen-tines, with-out
shad · do it,— Wait - er, bring me shad - roe. In shal-low shoals, Eng-lish

means, do it,— Peo-ple say, in Bos-ton, ev-en beans do it,—
soles do it,— Gold-fish, in the pri-va-cy of bowls, do it,—

Let's do it,— let's fall in_ love. 2. Ro-man-tic
Let's do it,— let's fall in_ love.

Lover, Come Back To Me!

"Cuando Vuelvas A Mí"

Words by
OSCAR HAMMERSTEIN 2nd
Spanish text by
JOHNNIE CAMACHO

Music by
SIGMUND ROMBERG

Publisher member of A. S. C. A. P.
International Copyright Secured.   *Made in U. S. A.*

met you Seems to stay for - ev - er in my mind.
tan - to, cuan - do quie - ras, vuel - ve jun - to_a mí.

REFRAIN

The sky was blue, And high a - bove The moon was new
El rui - se - ñor no can - ta ya; El cie - lo_a - zul

And so was love. This eag - er heart of mine was sing - ing:
se ha pues - to gris, y so - lo, se_a - bri - rán las flo - res,

"Lov - er, where can you be?" You came at last,
Cuan - do vuel - vas a mí. Mi co - ra - zón

walked a-long with you,
quel a-mor de a-yer

No won-der I am lone-ly.
por siem-pre en dul-ce cal-ma.

The sky is blue,
Tu en-con-tra-rás

The night is cold,
un cie-lo a-zul

The moon is new,
y un co-ra-zón

But love is old,
ya muy fe-liz;

And, while I'm wait-ing here,
y den-tro de mi ser,

This heart of mine is sing-ing:
ten-drás mi bien, re-fu-gio,

"Lov-er come back to me!"
Cuan-do vuel-vas a mí.

me!"
mí.

JEEPERS CREEPERS

Lyric by JOHNNY MERCER A.S.C.A.P. Music by HARRY WARREN A.S.C.A.P.

WARNER BROS.
Pictures Inc., Presents

"GOING PLACES"

WITH

DICK POWELL

ANITA LOUISE • RONALD REAGAN • ALLEN JENKINS
WALTER CATLETT • HAROLD HUBER
LOUIS ARMSTRONG • MAXINE SULLIVAN

Directed by RAY ENRIGHT
Music and Lyrics by Harry Warren and Johnny Mercer

Screen Play by Sig Herzig,
Jerry Wald & Maurice Leo
Based upon the play "The
Hottentot" by Victor Mapes
and William Collier, Sr.
A First National Picture

SAY IT WITH A KISS
JEEPERS CREEPERS
MUTINY IN THE NURSERY

M. WITMARK & SONS
NEW YORK

IT'S ONLY A PAPER MOON

FROM THE
PARAMOUNT PICTURE

TAKE A CHANCE

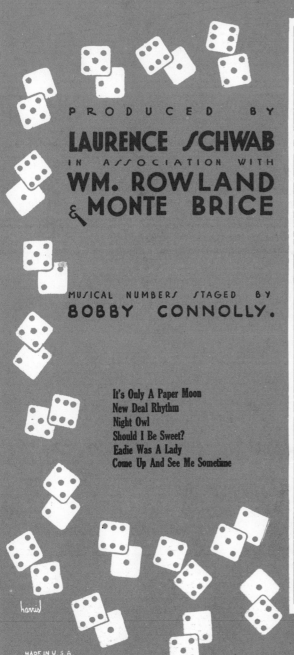

PRODUCED BY
LAURENCE SCHWAB
IN ASSOCIATION WITH
WM. ROWLAND
& MONTE BRICE

MUSICAL NUMBERS STAGED BY
BOBBY CONNOLLY.

It's Only A Paper Moon
New Deal Rhythm
Night Owl
Should I Be Sweet?
Eadie Was A Lady
Come Up And See Me Sometime

JUNE KNIGHT — BUDDY ROGERS

HARMS
NEW YORK
CHAPPELL & C? LTD
LONDON   SYDNEY

MADE IN U.S.A.

harris

BEI MIR BIST DU SCHÖN

(MEANS THAT YOU'RE GRAND)

FEATURED IN
"LOVE · HONOR
AND
BEHAVE"

A WARNER BROS. PICTURE

WITH

PRISCILLA LANE
WAYNE MORRIS
DICK FORAN

English Version by
SAMMY CAHN AND
SAUL CHAPLIN
A.S.C.A.P.

Original Lyrics by
JACOB JACOBS

Music by
SHOLOM SECUNDA

HARMS
INC
NEW YORK

When Day Is Done

American version based on the European success "MADONNA"

HARMS
INCORPORATED
NEW YORK

MADE IN U.S.A.

WORDS BY

B. G. De Sylva

MUSIC BY

Dr Robert Katscher

TIP TOE THROUGH THE TULIPS WITH ME

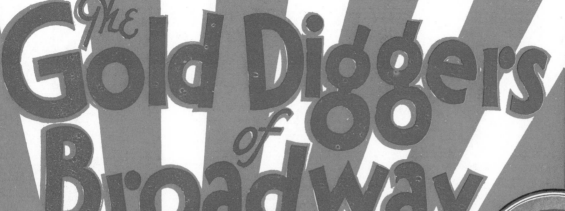

The Gold Diggers of Broadway

Lyrics by
AL DUBIN
BY ARRANGEMENT
WITH GENE, AUSTIN, INC.
Music by
JOE BURKE

Nancy Welford

Conway Tearle

Winnie Lightner

Ann Pennington

Lilyan Tashman

Nick Lucas

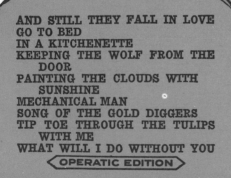

AND STILL THEY FALL IN LOVE
GO TO BED
IN A KITCHENETTE
KEEPING THE WOLF FROM THE
    DOOR
PAINTING THE CLOUDS WITH
    SUNSHINE
MECHANICAL MAN
SONG OF THE GOLD DIGGERS
TIP TOE THROUGH THE TULIPS
    WITH ME
WHAT WILL I DO WITHOUT YOU

OPERATIC EDITION

M. WITMARK & SONS
NEW YORK
Printed in U.S.A.

A WARNER BROS. VITAPHONE TALKING PICTURE

SOMETIMES I'M HAPPY

FROM VINCENT YOUMANS' HIT THE DECK

RADIO PICTURE'S
Screen Musical Comedy

STARRING
JACK OAKIE
POLLY WALKER
AND A BRILLIANT
SINGING CAST

BOOK BY
HERBERT FIELDS
ORIGINAL SCORE BY
LEO ROBIN & CLIFFORD GREY
MUSIC BY
VINCENT YOUMANS

Sometimes I'm Happy
Hallelujah!
The Harbor Of My Heart
Nothing Could Be Sweeter

HARMS
INCORPORATED
NEW YORK
CHAPPELL & Co LTD.
LONDON   SYDNEY

MADE IN U.S.A.

JUST ONE OF THOSE THINGS

E. RAY GOETZ PRESENTS

THE
NEW YORKERS

I'm Getting Myself Ready For You
Where Have You Been?
Love For Sale
Just One Of Those Things
Let's Fly Away

BOOK BY
HERBERT FIELDS
BASED ON A STORY BY
PETER ARNO & E. RAY GOETZ
LYRICS & MUSIC BY
COLE PORTER

HARMS
INCORPORATED
NEW YORK
CHAPPELL & CO LTD
LONDON   SYDNEY

MADE IN U.S.A.

OF THEE I SING

MUSIC BY
GEORGE GERSHWIN

WORDS BY
IRA GERSHWIN

Chandler Cowles and Ben Segal
PRESENT

OF THEE I SING

BOOK BY
GEORGE S. KAUFMAN
AND MORRIE RYSKIND

DIRECTED BY
GEORGE S. KAUFMAN

DANCES AND MUSICAL NUMBERS BY
HELEN TAMARIS

OF THEE I SING
LOVE IS SWEEPING THE COUNTRY
MINE
BECAUSE, BECAUSE
WINTERGREEN FOR PRESIDENT
WHO CARES?

PRICE
60¢
IN U.S.A.

WHEN PERFORMING THIS COMPOSITION KINDLY GIVE ALL PROGRAM CREDITS TO
NEW WORLD MUSIC CORP.
HARMS, INC., SOLE SELLING AGENT
NEW YORK, N. Y.

PRINTED IN U.S.A.

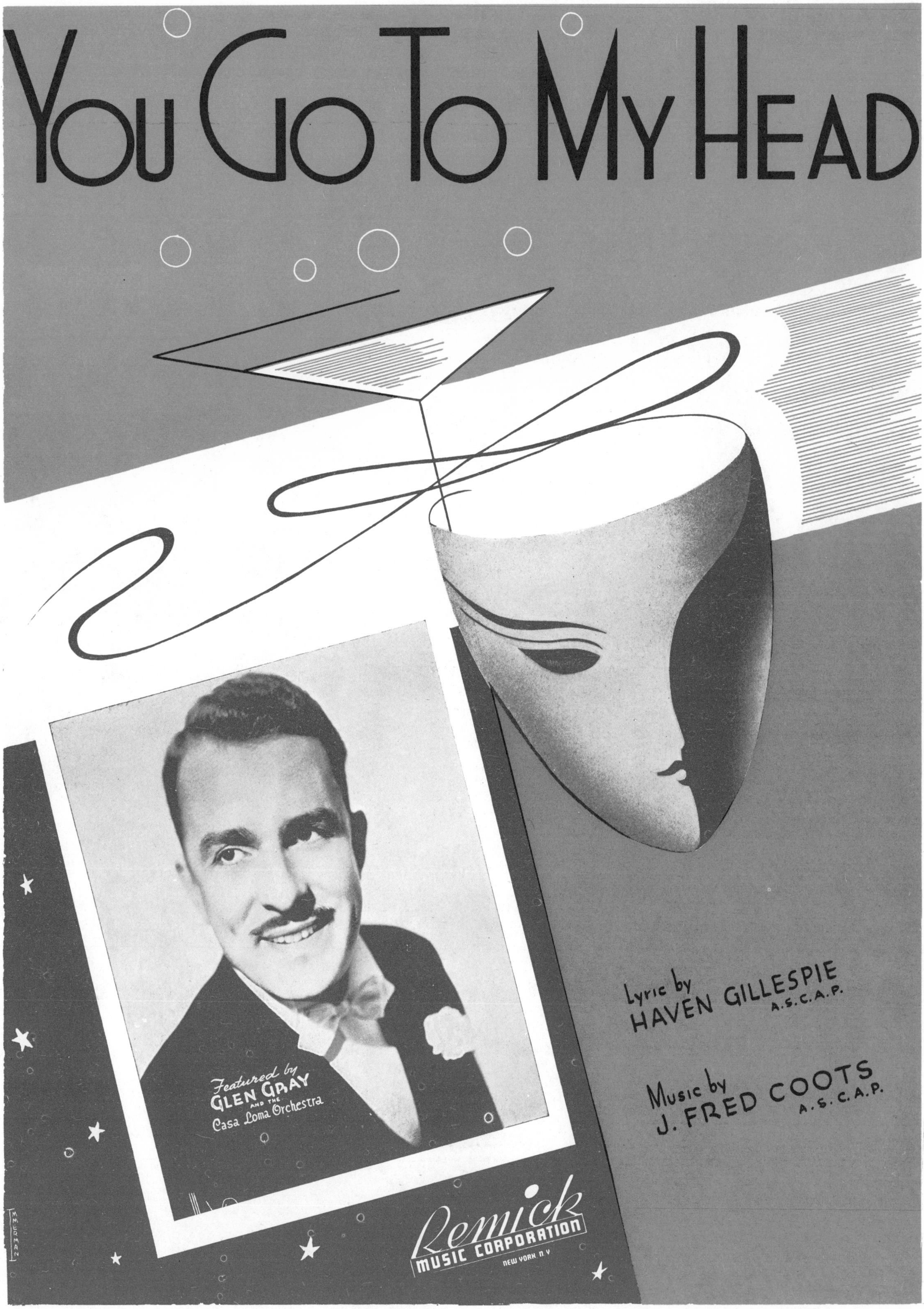

YOU GO TO MY HEAD
Featured by GLEN GRAY AND THE Casa Loma Orchestra
Lyric by HAVEN GILLESPIE A.S.C.A.P.
Music by J. FRED COOTS A.S.C.A.P.
Remick MUSIC CORPORATION NEW YORK, N.Y.

IF I COULD BE WITH YOU

(ONE HOUR TO-NIGHT)

SONG
WITH
UKULELE
ARRANGEMENT

by
HENRY CREAMER
And
JIMMY JOHNSON

SUCCESSFULLY FEATURED BY
Ruth Etting
ZIEGFELD STAR

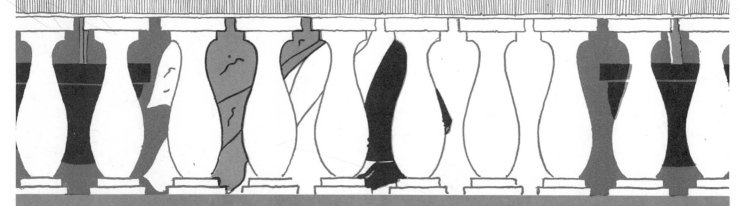

Remick Music Corp.
219 W. 46TH ST., New York

BABY FACE

Words and Music by
BENNY DAVIS
and
HARRY AKST

WHEN PERFORMING THIS COMPOSITION KINDLY GIVE ALL
PROGRAM CREDITS TO

Remick
MUSIC CORPORATION
NEW YORK, N.Y.

Price 50¢
in U. S. A.

TEA FOR TWO

California
Here I Come

with
UKULELE
ACCOMPANIMENT

Sung with Great Success by
AL JOLSON
in
BOMBO

Direction of MESSRS LEE & J.J. SHUBERT

M. WITMARK & SONS
NEW YORK

by AL. JOLSON
BUD DE SYLVA
and JOSEPH MEYER

PRINTED
IN U.S.A.

ANYTHING GOES
HENRY DUFFY PRESENTS
BY ARRANGEMENT WITH
VINTON FREEDLEY INC.
GEORGE MURPHY
SHIRLEY ROSS
HUGH O'CONNELL
IN
"ANYTHING GOES"
A NEW MUSICAL COMEDY
MUSIC BY
COLE PORTER
STORY BY
GUY BOLTON
AND
P.G. WODEHOUSE
STAGED BY
HOWARD LINDSAY
DANCES AND ENSEMBLES BY
ROBERT ALTON
ANYTHING GOES
BUDDIE BEWARE
YOU'RE THE TOP
ALL THROUGH THE NIGHT
GYPSY IN ME
BLOW, GABRIEL, BLOW
I GET A KICK OUT OF YOU
MADE IN U.S.A.
harris
HARMS
INCORPORATED
NEW YORK
CHAPPELL & Co LTD
LONDON
SYDNEY

FORTY-SECOND STREET

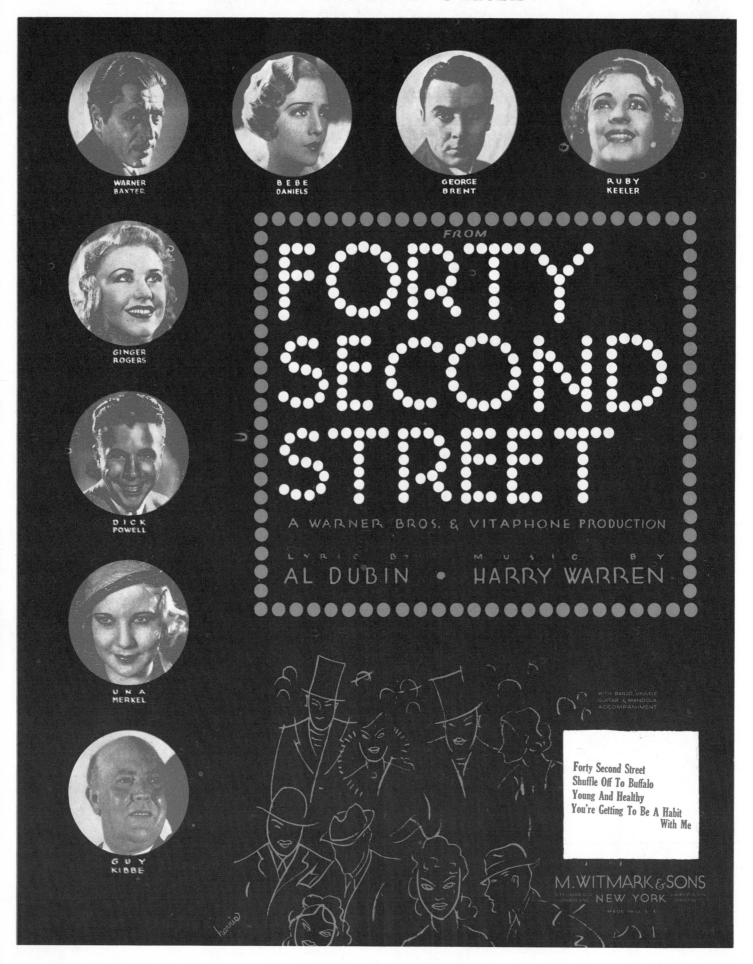

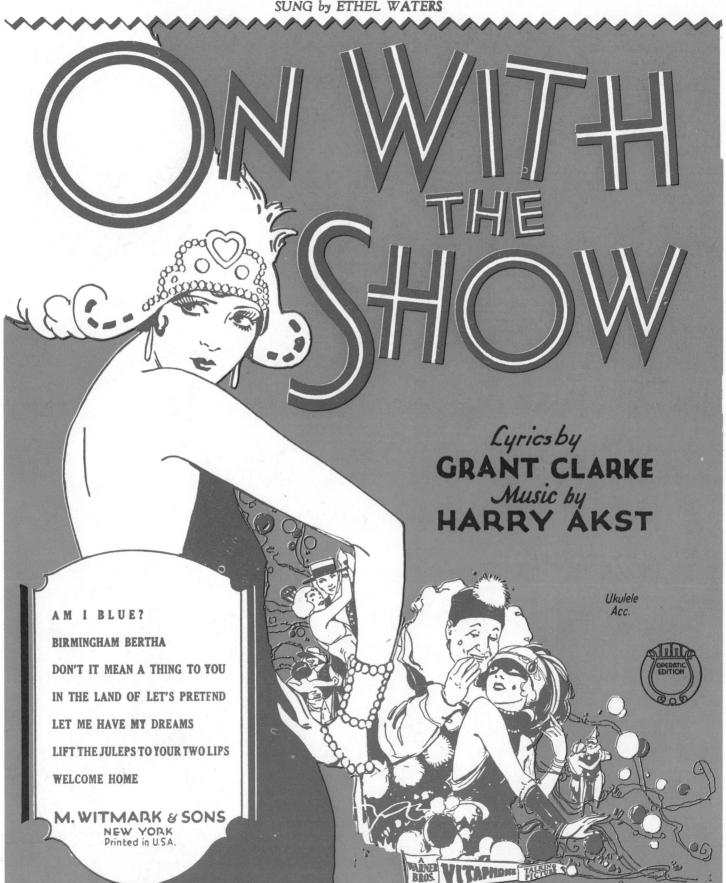

THOU SWELL

LEW FIELDS and LYLE D. ANDREWS
PRESENT
A MUSICAL ADAPTATION OF *MARK TWAIN'S*

A Connecticut Yankee

BOOK BY
HERBERT FIELDS
MUSIC BY
RICHARD RODGERS
LYRICS BY
LORENZ HART

My Heart Stood Still
I Feel At Home With You
Thou Swell
I Blush
On A Desert Island With You
Someone Should Tell Them
Selection

STAGED BY
ALEXANDER
LEFTWICH

DANCES BY
BUSBY
BERKELEY

ENTIRE PRODUCTION
UNDER SUPERVISION OF
LEW FIELDS

HARMS
INCORPORATED
NEW YORK

MADE IN U. S. A.

SHADOW WALTZ

WARNER BROS.
& THE VITAPHONE CORP.
present

Gold Diggers of 1933

with

WARREN WILLIAM • JOAN BLONDELL
ALINE MacMAHON • RUBY KEELER
DICK POWELL • GUY KIBBEE • GINGER ROGERS

words by
AL DUBIN • music by **HARRY WARREN**

directed by
MERVYN LE ROY
dances by
BUSBY BERKELEY

Shadow Waltz
Pettin' In The Park
Remember My Forgotten Man
I've Got To Sing A Torch Song
The Gold Diggers' Song
(We're In The Money)

Remick Music Corp.
1657 B'WAY., New York

B. FELDMAN & CO.   J. ALBERT & SON.
LONDON, ENG.   SYDNEY, AUST.
MADE IN U.S.A.

BYE BYE BLACKBIRD

Song
with Ukulele Arrangement

Lyric by
Mort Dixon
Music by
Ray Henderson

Jimmy Carr
The Doctor of Melody

Jerome H. Remick & Co.
New York   Detroit
MADE IN U.S.A.

I'LL STRING ALONG WITH YOU

Fair and Warmer
I'll String Along With You
Man On The Flying Trapeze
Out For No Good
What Are Your Intentions

FROM
"20 MILLION SWEETHEARTS"

A WARNER BROS. PICTURE FEATURING

DICK POWELL · GINGER ROGERS
PAT O'BRIEN · THE 4 MILLS BROTHERS
TED FIORITO AND HIS ORCHESTRA

WORDS BY
AL DUBIN
MUSIC BY
HARRY WARREN

M. WITMARK & SONS
NEW YORK
B. FELDMAN & CO., LONDON, ENG.
MADE IN U.S.A.

NAGASAKI

Words by
MORT DIXON

Music by
HARRY WARREN

Fel-lows if you're on
When the day is warm

I will spin a yarn
You can keep in form

That was told to me by a-ble sea-man Jones
With a bowl of rice be-neath a par-a-sol

Once he had the blues
Ev-'ry gen-tle-man

So he took a cruise
has to use a fan

Far a-way from night clubs
And they on-ly wear sus-

147

CHORUS

148

They kiss-ee and hug-ee nice__ By Jin-go! it's worth the price__
You must have to act your age__ Or wind up in-side a cage__

Back in Nag-a-sak-i where the fel-lers chew to-bac-cy And the wo-men wick-y wack-y woo

Fine

PATTER

With an ice cream cone and a bot-tle of tea You can rest all day by the hick-o-ry tree But when

night comes 'round Oh Gosh! Oh Gee! Moth-er, moth-er, moth-er pin a rose on me.

To Chos., Fine

Two Little Babes In The Wood

Words and Music by
COLE PORTER

There's a tale of two lit-tle or-phans who were left in their un-cle's care, To be

© MCMXXVIII by HARMS, INC.
Copyright Renewed

152

155

You Took Advantage Of Me

Words by
LORENZ HART

Music by
RICHARD RODGERS

men-tal de-fi-cient you'll grade me,____ I've giv-en you plen-ty of
hors-es are fre-quent-ly sil-ly,____ Mine ran from the beach of Ka-

da-ta.____ You came, you saw and you slayed me, And that-a is that-a!
lu-a,____ And left me a-lone for a fil-ly, So I-a picked you-a.

REFRAIN
Liltingly

I'm a sent-i-ment-al sap, that's all.___ What's the use of try-ing

not to fall?___ I have no will,__ You've made your kill__ 'Cause you

157

took ad-vant-age of me! I'm just like an ap-ple on a bough_ And you're gon-na shake me down some-how, So what's the use,_ you've cooked my goose_'Cause you took ad-vant-age of me! I'm so hot and both-ered that I don't know_ My el-bow from_ my

ear;_____ I suf-fer some-thing aw-ful each time you go_ And

much worse when–you're near. Here am I with all my bridg-es burned,–

Just a babe in arms where you're con-cerned,_ So lock the doors_ and

call me yours_'Cause you took ad-vant-age of me! me!

Am I Blue?

Lyric by
GRANT CLARKE

Music by
HARRY AKST

*Diagrams for Guitar, Symbols for Ukulele and Banjo

161

Can't We Be Friends?

Words by
PAUL JAMES

Music by
KAY SWIFT

I should have seen it,— Now— it's too late!

Refrain (Slowly and with much expression)

I thought I'd found the man of my dreams. Now it seems
I thought I knew the wheat from the chaff,— What a laugh!

This is how the sto-ry— ends: "He's goin' to turn me down and say,
This is how the sto-ry— ends: I let him turn me down and say,

"Can't we be friends?" I thought for once it
"Can't we be friends?" I act-ed like a

Happy Days Are Here Again

Words by
JACK YELLEN
a.s.c.a.p.

Music by
MILTON AGER
a.s.c.a.p.

Allegro moderato

So long, sad times! Go 'long, bad times! We are rid of you at last. How-dy, gay times! Clou-dy gray times, You are now a thing of the past._____ 'Cause

CHORUS

hap - py days___ are here a - gain.___ The
skies a - bove___ are clear a - gain.___ Let us
sing a song___ of cheer a - gain___ Hap - py days are
here a - gain!_____ Al - to - ge - ther

I May Be Wrong

But, I Think You're Wonderful!

Words by
HARRY RUSKIN

Music by
HENRY SULLIVAN

CHORUS

I may be wrong; but, I think you're won - der - ful!
I may be wrong; but, I think you're won - der - ful!

I may be wrong; but, I think you're swell!
I may be wrong; but, I think you're swell!
I like your

style; say, I think it's mar - vel - lous. I'm al - ways wrong so
style; say, I think it's mar - vel - lous. But I can't see so

how can I tell? All of __ my shirts are un - sight - ly
how can I tell? Deuc - es __ to me are all ac - es

Tip-Toe Thru' The Tulips With Me

Lyric by
AL DUBIN

Music by
JOE BURKE

REFRAIN

Tip-toe to the win-dow, by the win-dow, That is where I'll be, Come

tip-toe thru the tu-lips with me;

Tip-toe from your pil-low, to the sha-dow of a wil-low tree, And

tip-toe thru the tu-lips with me; Knee

deep_____ in flow-ers we'll stray___ We'll

keep_____ the show-ers a-way;___ And if I

kiss you in the gar-den, in the moon-light, Will you par-don me, Come tip-toe thru the

tu-lips with me. me.___

rit.

sffz

WITH A SONG IN MY HEART

Words by
LORENZ HART

Music by
RICHARD RODGERS

time .... Ev -'ry meet - ing's a mar - vel - ous pas - time You're in -
light .... Not a note of our mu - sic is played out, It will

creas-ing-ly sweet, So when-ev - er we hap-pen to meet _____ I greet you
be just as sweet, And an air that I'll live to re - peat: _____ I greet you

tacet

REFRAIN   Rather slow, but with rhythm

With a song in my heart. _____ I be-hold your a -

a tempo
p - mf

R.H.

dor - a - ble face,   Just a song at the start, _____

R.H.

178

You Do Something To Me

Words and Music by
COLE PORTER

THE THIRTIES

BODY AND SOUL

Words by
EDWARD HEYMAN
ROBERT SOUR and
FRANK EYTON

Music by
JOHNNY GREEN

Diagrams for Guitar, Symbols for Ukulele and Banjo

REFRAIN

(slowly, with expression)

My heart is sad and lone - ly, For you I sigh, for you, dear, on - ly. Why have - n't you seen it? I'm all for you, Bod - y and Soul! I spend my days in long - ing And won - d'ring why it's

looks like the end-ing Un - less I could have one more chance to prove, dear,

My life a wreck you're mak - ing, You know I'm yours for

just the tak-ing; I'd glad-ly sur - ren - der my-self to you, Bod-y and

Soul!

Soul!

But Not For Me

(Molly)

Tune Ukulele or Banjulele Banjo

A D F♯ B

Put Capo on 1st Fret

Words by
IRA GERSHWIN

Music by
GEORGE GERSHWIN

Old Man Sun-shine lis-ten, you! Nev-er tell me,

"Dreams come true!" Just try it And I'll start a ri-ot.

Letters over Uke diagrams are names of chords adaptable to Banjo or Guitar in original key.

Ukulele arr. by S. M. Zoltai

Bea-trice Fair-fax, don't you dare Ev-er tell me he will care; I'm

cer-tain It's the fin-al cur-tain, I nev-er want to

hear From an-y cheer-ful Pol-ly-an-nas, Who tell you

fate, Sup-plies a mate; It's all ba-na-nas! They're writ-ing
(He's knock-ing)

194

Can This Be Love?

Words by
PAUL JAMES

Music by
KAY SWIFT

Moderato

Piano

mf

rit.

Ukulele

G C E A

F   C+   F   Fmin.

p

p a tempo

Who knows why the sea   Or why the sky is

Bb7   C7   F   C7

blue?   Why should you love me,   Or

© 1930 by HARMS, INC.
Copyright Renewed
All Rights Reserved

I love you? Who knows how love

starts Or where its course will run?

Who knows why two hearts Will beat as one.

Refrain
I'm all at sea, Can this be love?

196

This mys-ter - y, Can this be love?—

I'm in a blue haze where noth-ing seems quite

real; I wan - der through days with

this cra - zy feel - ing What can it be, Can

From "SWEET AND LOW"

CHEERFUL LITTLE EARFUL

Words by
IRA GERSHWIN
and BILLY ROSE

Music by
HARRY WARREN

Ukulele
Bb Eb G C

I'm grow-ing tir-ed of lov-ey dove theme songs

That fif-ty mil-lion pia-nos pound _____

*Symbols for Guitar

Dancing On The Ceiling

(He Dances On My Ceiling)

Words by
LORENZ HART

Music by
RICHARD RODGERS

Dancing With Tears In My Eyes

Lyric by
AL DUBIN

Music by
JOE BURKE

Valse moderato

Vamp

Eb

Those who dance   and ro-mance   while they   dance,____   They seem   so
While the throng's   in the spell   of a   song,____   My thoughts keep

F♯ dim   **Fm**   **C+**

hap-py   and   gay;____   Tho' they sing   while they swing   and they
drift-ing   to   you;____   While each pair   seems to share   their af-

REFRAIN (*With feeling*)

Embraceable You

Words by
IRA GERSHWIN
French version by
Emelia Renaud

Spanish version by
JOHNNIE CAMACHO

Music by
GEORGE GERSHWIN

REFRAIN *Rhythmically*

Fine And Dandy

Words by
PAUL JAMES

Music by
KAY SWIFT

I GOT RHYTHM

Words by
IRA GERSHWIN

Music by
GEORGE GERSHWIN

tree sing Their day-ful of song, Why should-n't

we sing a-long?_____ I'm chip-per

all the day, Hap-py with my lot. How do I

get that way? Look at what I've got:

REFRAIN (*with abandon*)

I__ got rhy - thm, I__ got mu - sic,__

I__ got my man__ Who could ask for an - y - thing more?

I__ got dais - ies__ In green pas - tures,__ I__ got

my man Who could ask for an - y - thing more? Old__ Man

Bar 3rd fret with 1st finger and use 2nd and 3rd finger on remaining dots

I've Got A Crush On You

Duet

(Ann-Timothy)

Words by
IRA GERSHWIN

Music by
GEORGE GERSHWIN

LOVE FOR SALE

Words and Music by
COLE PORTER

226

REFRAIN (*with swinging rhythm and not fast*)

Who would like to sam-ple my sup - ply? _____ Who's pre-pared to

pay the price For a trip to par-a-dise? Love _____ for sale. _____

Let the po - ets pipe of love In their child-ish way,

I know ev-'ry type of love Bet-ter far than, they. If you want the

thrill of love, I've been thru the mill of love; Old love, new love,

Please Don't Talk About Me
When I'm Gone

Tune Ukulele
4   3   2   1
B♭ E♭ G C

By SIDNEY CLARE,
SAM H. STEPT
and BEE PALMER

Years we've been to - geth - er, Seems we can't get a - long;
Just be - fore our part - ing, Some-thing I __ want to say;

No mat-ter what I   do,   It don't ap-peal to   you.
I'm real-ly sor-ry   now,   For ev-'ry brok-en   vow.

Makes no diff-'rence wheth-er   I am right or I'm   wrong.
Sweet-heart, now you're start-ing On your own lit-tle way,

If we can't be   sweet-hearts,   This much you can   do:
One thing please re - mem - ber,   In your mind some - how!

REFRAIN

Please don't talk a - bout— me when I'm gone,_____ Oh, hon-ey,
though our friendship ceas - es, from now on;_____ And, lis - ten,
if you can't say an - y-thing real nice,_____ It's bet - ter
not to talk at all,— is my ad - vice._____ We're part - ing,

you go your way I'll go mine, it's best that we do;____

Here's a kiss! I hope that this brings lots of luck to you.

Makes no diff'rence how__ I car-ry on,_____ Re-mem-ber, please don't talk a-

-bout me when I'm gone.   gone._____

Something To Remember You By

Words by
HOWARD DIETZ

Music by
ARTHUR SCHWARTZ

Molto moderato

VOICE

PIANO

You are leav-ing me, and

I will try to face the world a - lone.

What will be will be, but time can-not e - rase the love we've known.

TEN CENTS A DANCE

Words by
LORENZ HART

Music by
RICHARD RODGERS

that the pal-ace fea-tures At ex-act-ly a dime a throw.

poco rit.

REFRAIN— **Slowly, quasi rubato**

Ten cents a dance; That's what they pay me. Gosh, how they weigh me

down! Ten cents a dance, Pan-sies and rough guys,

Tough guys who tear my gown! Sev-en to mid-night, I hear drums,

Loud-ly the sax-o-phone blows, Trum-pets are tear-ing my ear-drums.

poco cresc.

239

Would You Like To Take A Walk

(Sump'n Good'll Come From That)

Lyric by
MORT DIXON &
BILLY ROSE

Music by
HARRY WARREN

Moderato

I saw you stroll-ing by your sol-i - tar-y Am I nose-y ver-y
My lit-tle heart is full of pal-pi - ta-tion What I need is con-so-

ver - y I'd like to bet a juic-y huck-le - ber-ry What you're af - ter is a
-la-tion I'd like to stage a lit-tle cel-e - bra-tion In the moon-light right a-

gal We're both in luck for in - tro - duc - tions are not nec - es - sa - ry.
- way I'll feel all pep't if you'll ac - cept my friend - ly in - vi - ta - tion.

CHORUS

Mm - Mm - Mm Would you like to take a walk? Mm - Mm - Mm Do you

think it's gon - na rain? Mm - Mm - Mm How a - bout a sas - par - il - la?

Gee the moon is yel - ler Sum - p'n good - 'll come from that

Bidin' My Time

Words by
IRA GERSHWIN

Music by
GEORGE GERSHWIN

Some fel-lers love to "Tip-Toe Through the Tu-lips;"

Some fel-lers go on "Sing — ing In The Rain."

Some fel-lers keep on "Paint-in' Skies With Sun-Shine."

*Letters over UKE diagrams are names of chords
adaptable to Banjo or Guitar in original key*

Ukulele Arr. by
S. M. ZOLTAI

247

I FOUND A MILLION DOLLAR BABY

(IN A FIVE AND TEN CENT STORE)

Lyric by
BILLY ROSE and
MORT DIXON

Music by
HARRY WARREN

Love comes a-long like a pop-u-lar song, An-y-time or an-y-where at
Love used to be quite a stran-ger to me Did-n't know a sen-ti-men-tal

all. Rain or sun-shine, spring or fall,
word, Thoughts of kiss-ing seemed ab-surd.

*Diagrams for Guitar, Symbols for Ukulele and Banjo

Five And Ten Cent Store; The rain con-tin-ued for an

hour, — I hung a-round for three or four,

A-round a mil-lion dol-lar ba-by In a Five and Ten Cent

Store. She was sell-ing chi-na And when she made those

eyes _____ I kept buy-ing chi - na ___ un-til the crowd got

wise _____ In - ci-dent'-ly, If you should run in-to a show-er,

Just step in-side my cot - tage door And meet the mil - lion dol - lar

ba - by From the Five and Ten Cent Store! ___ Store! ___

I've Got Five Dollars

(DUET: Geraldine and Michael)

Words by
LORENZ HART

Music by
RICHARD RODGERS

He: Mis-ter Shy-lock was stin-gy;— I was mis-er-ly,
She: Peg-gy Joyce_ has a busi-ness,_ All her hus-bands have

too. I was more self-ish And crab-by than a shell-fish,
gold. And Lil-yan Tash-man Is not kissed by an ash-man;

*Letters over Uke diagrams are names of chords
adaptable to Banjo or Guitar in original key.

Ukulele Arr. by
S. M. ZOLTAI

Oh dear,_ it's queer_ What love_ can do!
But now,_ some-how_ Wealth leaves_ me cold.

I'd give all_ my pos-ses-sions for you: _____
Though you're poor_ as a church mouse_ I'm sold! _____

Refrain

He: I've got five dol-lars; I'm in good con-
She: I've got five dol-lars; Eight-y five re-

di-tion; And I've got am-bi-tion; That be-longs to
la-tions; Two lace com-bi-na-tions; They be-long to

OF THEE I SING

Words by
IRA GERSHWIN

Music by
GEORGE GERSHWIN

WHEN YOUR LOVER HAS GONE

Words and Music by
E. A. SWAN

*Diagrams for Guitar, Symbols for Ukulele and Banjo

You're My Everything

Featured in the 20th Century-Fox Picture
"YOU'RE MY EVERYTHING"

Words by
MORT DIXON
and JOE YOUNG

Music by
HARRY WARREN

Lyrics: I'm so a-shamed of my vo-cab-u-la-ry, It is-n't what it real-ly ought to be. I

*Diagrams for Guitar, Symbols for Ukulele and Banjo

have a task that is-n't or-di-na - ry, When

I'm des-crib-ing what you are to me. Can't you see,

Refrain
Slowly, with much expression

You're my ev - 'ry-thing_____ un-der-neath the sun,_____

You're my ev - 'ry-thing_____ rolled up in - to

264

APRIL IN PARIS
"Avril à Paris"

Words by
E. Y. HARBURG
French version by
EMELIA RENAUD

Music by
VERNON DUKE

A-pril's in the air, But here in Par-is A-pril wears a dif-f'rent gown.
A-vril est dans l'air I-ci à Pa-ris La na-ture a re-vê-tue

You can see her waltz-ing down the street. The tang of
U-ne toi-let-te pour son dé-but. Un bou-quet

wine is in the air, I'm drunk with all the hap-pi-ness that Spring can give,
de vin est dans l'air Et tout ce bon-heur du Prin-temps nous en - i - vre

Nev - er dreamed it could be so ex - cit-ing to live._____
Nous i - gno - rions qu'il fai-sait si bon de vi - vre._____

REFRAIN *amoroso*

A - pril in Par - is,_____ Chest-nuts in blos - som,___
A - vril à Pa - ris,_____ Châ - tai - gniers fleu - ris ___

p-mf amoroso

Hol - i - day ta - bles un - der the trees.___
Tout est en fê - te sous la feuil - lée.___

Brother, Can You Spare A Dime?

Words by
E. Y. HARBURG

Music by
JAY GORNEY

building a dream   With peace and glory a - head _____ Why should

I be stand-ing in   line   just wait-ing for   bread?

Refrain
mp-f (with much expression)
Once I built a rail-road, made it run,__ Made it race a-gainst time.

Once I built a rail-road,   Now it's done __   Broth-er can you spare a   dime?

Forty Second Street

Words by
AL DUBIN

Music by
HARRY WARREN

Symbols for Guitar and Banjo.

runs in-to Times Square.___ A cra-zy quilt that

Wall Street "Jack" built, If you've got a lit-tle

time to spare, I want to take you there.___

Refrain Come and meet___ those danc-ing feet,___ On the

276

I Guess I'll Have To Change My Plan

Words by
HOWARD DIETZ

Music by
ARTHUR SCHWARTZ

✲ *Open strings*

self up-on the shelf, and that was that___ I tried to
try to be a fly Lo-tha-ri-o!___ I think I'll

reach the moon but when I got there, All that I could
crawl right back and in-to my shell, Dwell-ing in my

get was the air, My feet are back up-on the ground___ I've lost the
per-son-al H-ll. I'll have to change my plan a-round___ I've lost the

one girl I found. I
one girl I found.

LOUISIANA HAYRIDE

Words and Music by
HOWARD DIETZ and
ARTHUR SCHWARTZ

What kind o' fun do yo' fan-cy mos'?__ Pic-nic?__ (No ma'am!__) Oys-ter sup-per? (No ma'am!__) Straw-ber-ry fes-ti-val? (No ma'am!__) What kind o' fun do yo' fan-cy mos'?__(Yo' have-n't hit it yet, but yo' might-y close!__) Don't hold it back an-y lon-ger!_ Is it hay-ride?__ (Yes ma'am!__)

REFRAIN

Get go-in', Lou-is-i-an-a hay-ride! Get go-in', we all is read-y!

Start sum-pin', Lou-is-i-an-a hay-ride! No use fo' call-in' de roll. Oh, I

like dat sport; Sit-tin' in de hay! Lov-in' it a-way, Oh, Oh! Fo' de

time is short, crack yo' lit-tle whip! Get yo' lit-tle ship to go.____

NIGHT AND DAY

French version by
EMÉLIA RENAUD
Spanish Text by
JOHNNIE CAMACHO

Words and Music by
COLE PORTER

289

A Shine On Your Shoes

Words and Music by
HOWARD DIETZ and
ARTHUR SCHWARTZ

Symbols for Guitar and Banjo

Publisher member of A. S. C. A. P.
International Copyright Secured. *Made in U. S. A.*

If you want to get em-ploy-ment Tid-y up your fac-es and a-mount to sum-thin',

Those big men who got up there___ all de-clare:___

Refrain

When there's a shine on your shoes, There's a mel-o-dy in your

heart, With a sing-a-ble hap-py feel-ing, A

fer-ry boat, While the wat-er's go-ing "wish-y-wash-y - wish-y-wash-y-wish-y-wash-y-

woo!" _____ But it does-n't mat-ter where you

get it,___ It-'ll do a lot of good if you let it;___ A

lit-tle bit of pol-ish will a - bol-ish what's both-er-ing you. _____

D.S. al Fine
(Back to Refrain)

You're An Old Smoothie

Words by
B.G. DE SYLVA

Music by
RICHARD A. WHITING
and HERB BROWN NACIO

Moderato

rit

Piano

p a tempo

Tune Uke
4 3 2 1
G C E A

C   A7   D7

You're the smooth-est so and so,— Not on-ly that, you're might-y— cute; You're

Emi.   G aug.   C   D7   G7

slick - er, far,— than the trous-ers are,— Of my last year's blue serge suit.

sf

* *Symbols for Guitar and Banjo*

I'm the soft-est so and so __ that an-y girl-ie ev-er knew, Oh, I

may be dumb __ as they ev-er come, __ But at least, I'm on to you!

Refrain

You're __ an old smooth-ie, __ I'm __ an old soft-ie; __

I'm just like put-ty in the hands of a girl like

You. You're_ an old mean - ie,_ I'm_ a big

boob - ie,_ I just go nut - ty, in the hands of a

girl like you. Poor me, you

played me for a sap; Poor you, you thought you'd laid a trap!

You're Getting To Be A Habit With Me

Words by
AL DUBIN

Music by
HARRY WARREN

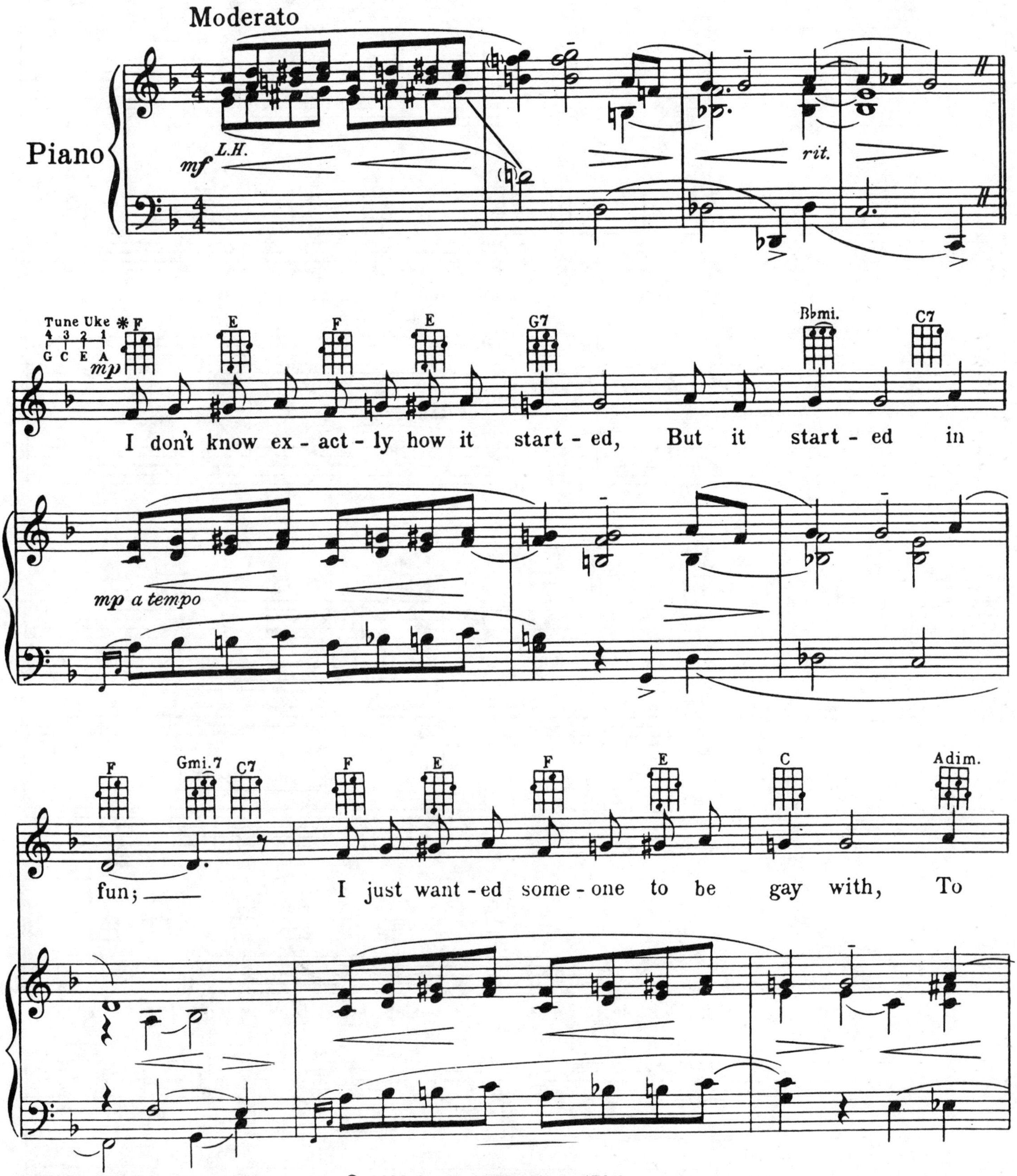

Moderato
Piano
mf L.H.
rit.
Tune Uke
4 3 2 1
G C E A
* F E F E G7 Bbmi. C7
mp
I don't know exactly how it started, But it started in
mp a tempo
F Gmi.7 C7 F E F E C Adim.
fun; I just wanted someone to be gay with, To

* Symbols for Guitar and Banjo.

Young And Healthy

Words by
AL DUBIN

Music by
HARRY WARREN

Allegretto

Piano

I know a bun-dle of hu-man-i-ty, She's a-bout so high; ___ I'm near-ly driv-en to in-san-i-ty,

Symbols for Guitar and Banjo.

It would real-ly be a sin not to have you in my arms. I'm young and health-y, And so are you; When the moon is in the sky, tell me, what am I to do? If I could hate "yuh,"

I Cover The Waterfront

Words by
EDWARD HEYMAN

Music by
JOHNNY GREEN

*Diagrams for Guitar, Symbols for Ukulele and Banjo

Are you for-get-ting? Do you re-mem-ber? Will you re-turn?

I cov-er the wat-er-front,— I'm watch-ing the

sea, For the one I love— must soon come back— to

me.

me.

It's Only A Paper Moon

Words by
BILLY ROSE and
E. Y. HARBURG

Music by
HAROLD ARLEN

SHADOW WALTZ

Words by
AL. DUBIN

Music by
HARRY WARREN

★ Symbols for Guitar and Banjo

Here am I, where are you?

REFRAIN *con espressione*
In the shad-ows, let me come and sing to you,

Let me dream a song that I can bring to you; Take me in your arms and

let me cling to you, Let me lin-ger long, let me live my song.

In the win-ter, let me bring the spring to you,

Let me feel that I mean ev-'ry-thing to you;____ Love's old song____ will be

new,____ In the shad-ows,when I come and sing to you.____

you, dear, In the shadows,when I come and sing to you.____

THE GOLD DIGGERS' SONG
(WE'RE IN THE MONEY)

Words by
AL. DUBIN

Music by
HARRY WARREN

Allegro moderato

Gone are my blues, And gone are my tears;

I've got good news To shout in your ears.

The sil-ver dol-lar has re-turned to the fold,___ With

Anything Goes

Words and Music by
COLE PORTER

*Symbols for Ukulele, Tenor-Guitar and Banjo

Lyrics: Times have changed____ And we've of-ten re-wound the clock____ Since the Pu-ri-tans got a shock____

When they land-ed on Ply-mouth Rock;___ If to-

day___ A - ny shock they should try to stem,___

'Stead of land-ing on Ply-mouth Rock, Ply-mouth Rock would land on them.___

REFRAIN

Autumn In New York

Words and Music by
VERNON DUKE

It's time to end my lone-ly hol-i-day — And bid the coun-try a has-ty fare-well. So on this gray and mel-an-

* *Symbols for Ukulele, Tenor-Guitar and Banjo*

REFRAIN

p-mf (liltingly and freely)

Au-tumn in New York, ___ Why does it seem so in - vit - ing?
Au-tumn in New York, ___ The gleaming roof-tops at sun - down.

Au-tumn in New York, ___ It spells the thrill of first night - ing,
Au-tumn in New York, ___ It lifts you up when you're run - down,

Glit-ter - ing crowds and shim-mer - ing clouds in can-yons of steel, ___ They're
Jad-ed rou - és and gay di - vorc-ees who lunch at the Ritz, ___ Will

mak-ing me feel ___ I'm home. ___ It's Au-tumn in New York, ___
tell you that "it's ___ di - vine!" ___ This Au-tumn in New York ___

I GET A KICK OUT OF YOU

Words and Music by
COLE PORTER

You May Not Be An Angel, But
I'll String Along With You

Lyrics by
AL. DUBIN

Music by
HARRY WARREN

All my life I wait-ed for an an-gel,_____ But no an-gel ev-er came a-long._____ Then one hap-py af-ter-noon I met you,_____

336

And my heart be-gan to sing a song,_____ Some-how, I mis-took you for an

an - gel, But now I'm glad that I was wrong:_____

REFRAIN

You may not be an an-gel, 'Cause an-gels are so few,

You And The Night And The Music
"Si Tú Pudieras Quererme"

Words by
HOWARD DIETZ
Spanish version by
Johnnie Camacho

Music by
ARTHUR SCHWARTZ

Song is in the air, Tell-ing us ro-mance is ours to share.
Lle-vo pre-so en mi, un se-cre-to fiél que es pa - ra tí;

Now at last we've found one an-oth-er a - lone.
Ten-go mu-chas co-sas que quie-ro de-cir.

You're A Builder Upper

Words by
IRA GERSHWIN and
E. Y. HARBURG

Music by
HAROLD ARLEN

When you want to, you are a-ble To make me feel that I'm Clark Ga-ble;

Then, next min-ute, you make me feel I'm some-thing from the Zoo.

* *Symbols for Ukulele, Tenor-Guitar and Banjo*

First you warm up, then you're dis-tant; Nev-er knew a girl so in-con-sis-tent. I'm a big shot, at half past one, A so-and-so, by two;__ Heav-en for-give you for your sins,__ Keep-ing me on nee-dles and pins!__

REFRAIN

p-f (not too fast)

You're a build-er up-per, a break-er down-er; A hold-er out-er, and I'm a giv-er in - er. Sad, but true, I'm a sap-a-roo, too, Tak-ing it from a tak-er o-ver like you. Don't know where I'm at - a, I'm just a this - a, Then I'm a

stooge for your charms.____ You're a build-er up-per, a

break-er down-er,____ A hold-er out-er, and I'm a giv-er

in - er. Sad, but true, I love it, I do!____

Be-ing brok-en by a build-er up-per like you.____ up-per like you.____

YOU'RE THE TOP

Words and Music by
COLE PORTER

REFRAIN

if this dit-ty Is not so pret-ty At least it-'ll tell you how great you are.

You're the top!
You're the top!
You're the Col-os-se-um,
You're Ma-hat-ma Ghan-di,

You're the top!
You're the top!
You're the Louvr' Mu-se-um,
You're Na-po-leon bran-dy,

You're a mel-o-dy
You're the pur-ple light
From a sym-pho-ny
Of a sum-mer night
by
in

Strauss, You're a Ben-del bon-net, A Shake-speare son-net, You're Mick-y Mouse.
Spain, You're the Na-tion'l Gall'-ry, You're Gar-bo's sal-'ry, You're cel-o-phane,

JUST ONE OF THOSE THINGS

Words and Music by
COLE PORTER

352

REFRAIN

"Don't for-get to drop a line to me, please," As Jul-iet cried in her Ro-meo's ear, "Ro-meo, why not face the fact, my dear?"

It was just one of those things, Just one of those cra-zy flings. One of those bells that now and then rings,

Zing! Went The Strings Of My Heart

Words and Music by
JAMES F. HANLEY

I still re-call the thrill, I guess I al-ways will,— I hope 'twill nev-er de-part,_____ Dear, with your lips to mine _ A rhap-so - dy di-vine.— Zing! went the strings of my heart.

heart._____

WHEN MY DREAM BOAT COMES HOME

Tune Ukulele

G C E A

Words and Music by
CLIFF FRIEND and
DAVE FRANKLIN
A.S.C.A.P.

Symbols for Guitar & Banjo, Frames for Ukulele

roam, _____ I will meet you _____ and greet you, _____ Hold you close-ly, _____ "My own," _____ Moon-lit wa-ters _____ will sing _____ of the ten-der love _____ you bring, _____ We'll be sweet-hearts _____ for-ev-er, _____ WHEN MY DREAM-BOAT _____ COMES HOME. WHEN MY _____ HOME. _____

BEI MIR BIST DU SCHÖN

(Means That You're Grand)

Original Lyrics by
JACOB JACOBS
Music by SHOLOM SECUNDA

English Version by
SAMMY CAHN and
SAUL CHAPLIN
A.S.C.A.P.

Of all the {girls}{boys} I've known,_ and I've known some,_ Un-til I

first met you_ I was lone - some,_ And when you came in sight,_ dear, my

*Diagrams for Guitar, Symbols for Ukulele and Banjo

heart grew light___ And this old world seemed___ new to me,
You're real-ly swell I have___ to ad-mit, you___ de-serve ex-
pres-sions that___ real-ly fit you,___ And so I've racked my brain,___ hop-ing
to ex - plain___ all the things that you___ do to me;

REFRAIN

Am

*"BEI MIR BIST DU SCHÖN,"__ Please let me ex - plain,__

F7 E7

"BEI MIR BIST DU SCHÖN" means that you're grand,__

F7 E7 Am

F7 E7 Am

"BEI MIR BIST DU SCHÖN,"__ A - gain I'll ex - plain,__

F7 E7 Am B7-5 E7

Boy: It means you're the fair - est in __ the land, __
Girl: It means that my heart's at your com - mand, __

* Pronounced "By Meer Bist Doo Shane"

364

Too Marvelous For Words

Lyric by
JOHNNY MERCER

Music by
RICHARD A. WHITING

Jeepers Creepers

From the First National Picture "GOING PLACES"

Lyric by
JOHNNY MERCER, *A.S.C.A.P.*

Music by
HARRY WARREN, *A.S.C.A.P.*

I don't care what the weath-er man says, When the weath-er man says it's rain-ing, You'll nev-er hear me com-plain-ing, I'm cer-tain the sun will shine, I don't care how the

* *Diagrams for Guitar, Symbols for Ukulele and Banjo*

weath - er vane points, When the weath - er vane points to gloom - y, It's

got - ta be sun - ny to me, When your eyes look in - to mine;

REFRAIN
(with a swing)

Jeep - ers Creep - ers! Where'd ya get those peep - ers?__

Jeep - ers Creep - ers! Where'd ya get those eyes?

You Go To My Head

Lyric by
HAVEN GILLESPIE
A.S.C.A.P.

Music by
J. FRED COOTS
A.S.C.A.P.

*Diagrams for Guitar, Symbols for Ukulele and Banjo

YOU GO TO MY HEAD __ like a sip of spark-ling

Bur-gun-dy brew __ and I find the ver-y men-tion of you __

like the kick-er in a ju-lep or two. _____ The

thrill of the thought __ that you might give a thought __ to my

374

You Must Have Been A Beautiful Baby

From the Warner Bros. Picture
"HARD TO GET"

Lyric by
JOHNNY MERCER, *A.S.C.A.P.*

Music by
HARRY WARREN, *A.S.C.A.P.*

Does your moth-er re-al-ize, The stork de-liv-ered quite a prize, The day he left you on the fam-'ly tree, Does your dad ap-pre-ci-ate, That you are mere-ly su-per great, The mir-a-cle of an-y cen-tu-

* *Diagrams for Guitar, Symbols for Ukulele and Banjo*

Heaven Can Wait

Lyric by
EDDIE DE LANGE
A.S.C.A.P.

Music by
JIMMY VAN HEUSEN
A.S.C.A.P.

There are a mil-lion plac-es, I know i could be. But I'd e-ven give up heav-en just to have you here with me.

*Diagrams for Guitar, Symbols for Ukulele and Banjo

INDEXES

ALPHABETICAL TITLE INDEX

CHORUS LINE INDEX

FIRST LINE INDEX

INDEX OF COMPOSERS AND LYRICISTS